Lest We Forget

Fred Seiker visits the school annually to talk about his experiences. to 6th Form Key Skills pupils.

To Elizabeth, my wife and friend.
Thank you for being there.

My gratitude also to all those who
supported and encouraged me.

Lest We Forget

THE RAILROAD OF DEATH

Sketches of Japanese atrocities carried out by Japanese military during the building of the Thai-Burma railroad by

ALLIED PRISONERS OF WAR 1942-1945

By Fred Seiker.

First Edition - 1995
Second Edition - 2002

Published by
Bevere Vivis Gallery Books Limited
Bevere Lane, Worcester WR3 7RQ UK
Tel: 01905 451291
Fax: 01905 454104
ISBN 0 9526987 2 2

Email: books@beverevivis.com
www.beverevivis.com/books/lestweforget/

Printed by Record Printers Limited
The Old Chapel, Pump Street, Bromyard, Herefordshire, UK
Tel: 01885 483653

CONTENTS

THE RAILROAD OF DEATH

Statistics

Number of Allied P.O.W.'s according to British records was
61,700

consisting of:
30,000 British
13,000 Australians
18,000 Dutch
700 Americans

The Japanese claim the total number of P.O.W.'s was
68,888

Total deaths
18,000

Approximate percentage of P.O.W.'s death toll was
30%

Many more were left behind in unknown shallow jungle graves

Many thousands suffered life disablement, physical and/or mental

Total length of Railroad was
415 km (260 miles)

Railroad was started in June 1942

Completed at Konkuita, Thailand, on 17 October 1943

Entire Railroad built in just 16 months

Based on the above figures one P.O.W. died every 23 metres. (75 ft) of track built

FOREWORD

I am grateful to Fred Seiker for the opportunity to write this foreword, which I do in my capacity as Chairman of the Soldiers', Sailors' and Airmen's Families Association and Forces Help Society for Worcestershire.

We have remembered in this year, 1995, the 50th anniversary of VE and VJ Day, both anniversaries rekindling painful memories and raising powerful emotions for those who experienced war. It has been an occasion too for the younger generation to learn a little of the sacrifices which were made by so many to enable us all to enjoy the freedoms of today.

This small, but important, book of drawings will have a profound effect on all who see them. They show with stark clarity what Fred Seiker and his fellow prisoners of war experienced daily, but of which so little was really known and understood worldwide. Fred does not use artist's licence, he shows only what he himself saw or experienced. I hope that this very special and personal account will remind us both of the heroism of those who were forced to work as slave labourers and of the terrible inhumanity to man, which existed then and which, perhaps, lurks dangerously beneath the surface of even our modern world.

Dermot B-H-Blundell
Brigadier (Retd) Late Grenadier Guards
1995

AUTHOR'S COMMENTS

At the time of the VJ 50th anniversary commemorations in August 1995 I held an exhibition at the Bevere Vivis Gallery in Worcester, entitled 'Lest We Forget'. The watercolour sketches, based on memory, represent either personal experiences or witnessed events during my time as a POW of the Japanese from 1942 to 1945. I have been urged by numerous people to assemble the collection of sketches into a published form so that the message contained in the paintings would not be forgotten.

I had for many years harboured a quiet anger at the way in which the Burma and the Thai railway war theatre were, almost deliberately, ignored by various governments. I wanted to show people what really happened during that dreadful period, particularly the younger generation. If I could alert them to the dangers of appeasement at all cost, then perhaps a repeat of such an horrendous crime could be averted. The public reception of my exhibition was beyond anything I expected. To witness the emotions, sadness and often outright anger was a very moving experience for me. It convinced me that perhaps a compilation of my sketches in the form of a book would be a worthwhile enterprise. Another contributory factor was the interest that local media expressed. My story and exhibition were widely reported in newspapers, on radio and television.

The atrocities depicted in my sketches are just some of the inhuman practices carried out by the Japanese as a matter of course, or just plain amusement. Many Allied POWs are still today suffering from mental and physical disorders. After many years of peace and civilised living the nightmares continue. In my opinion anyone having survived the Railway of Death is a special kind of person. Such a person has experienced and witnessed the most degrading behaviour by one human being to another. At the same time he has felt the power of the unconquerable spirit of civilised man. It is for this reason that, in a strange way, I feel priviliged to have experienced and survived the building of the Thai-Burma railroad. I have seen humanity at its very best and at the same time at its very nadir. I have seen men of stature in civil life crumble like dry earth, devoid of self-respect and concern for others. But I have also seen little men of ordinary backgrounds suddenly emerge as fearless leaders and giants of mental strength.

I am often asked by well meaning people whether I can forgive or forget. The question of forgiving is perhaps one of religious belief and conscience, but to forget is a dangerous road to tread. It is impossible to make those who have not endured the railroad understand this. It is a very personal and private experience - impossible to share with even your closest confidante. Nothing that life throws at a survivor of the Thai-Burma railroad can ever be as daunting as the building of the Railway of Death.

FORGET? NEVER!

I have donated all my original paintings to the National Memorial Arboretum at Alrewas, Staffordshire, U.K. where they are on permanent exhibition.

Fred Seiker was born in Rotterdam, Holland, in 1915. His elementary and further education were accomplished in Rotterdam, culminating in obtaining a place at the Rotterdam College of Marine Engineering. He served in the Dutch Merchant Navy before and during the war. In peacetime he mainly served on ships plying the Far East, South Africa, Canada and the eastern seaboard of the USA. In wartime he served on the North Atlantic routes and between the Far East and the United Kingdom.

In 1942 Fred found himself caught up in the Japanese invasion of Java. Unable to leave the island he volunteered into the Dutch Armed Forces on Java and subsequently became a prisoner of war of the Japanese. He was shipped out to Changi jail in Singapore, from where he was sent to Thailand to work as a slave labourer on the infamous Railroad of Death. He spent the remainder of the war years on the railway and managed to survive.

Despite the war ending on the 15th August 1945, the Dutch POW contingent was not repatriated to Holland until May 1946! That same year Fred arrived in England for the purpose of settling in the UK. He has lived here ever since and has no regrets. After a year of recuperation he set out to build a career in engineering. He worked in various capacities with well known engineering organisations and concluded his career at Project Management level.

After his retirement in 1985 he and his wife Elizabeth moved to Worcester. Fred took up painting as a hobby and is now an accomplished watercolour artist. His usual work covers landscapes, boats, buildings and associated subjects. He has his own style, entirely different from the line expressions depicted in his POW sketches.

Plate 1

'FIT' PARADE
MS.

Plate 3

TIED TO TREE WITH
BARBED WIRE FOR 48HRS.
WITHOUT FOOD OR WATER.
BUCKET OF WATER IN FRONT OF HIM.
MS.

P.O.W. IS SUSPENDED BY THUMBS
WITH TOES JUST TOUCHING GROUND.

Plate 5

MADE TO KNEEL ON SHARP EDGED TIMBERS.
CARRYING HEAVY BOULDER UP TO 3 HRS.

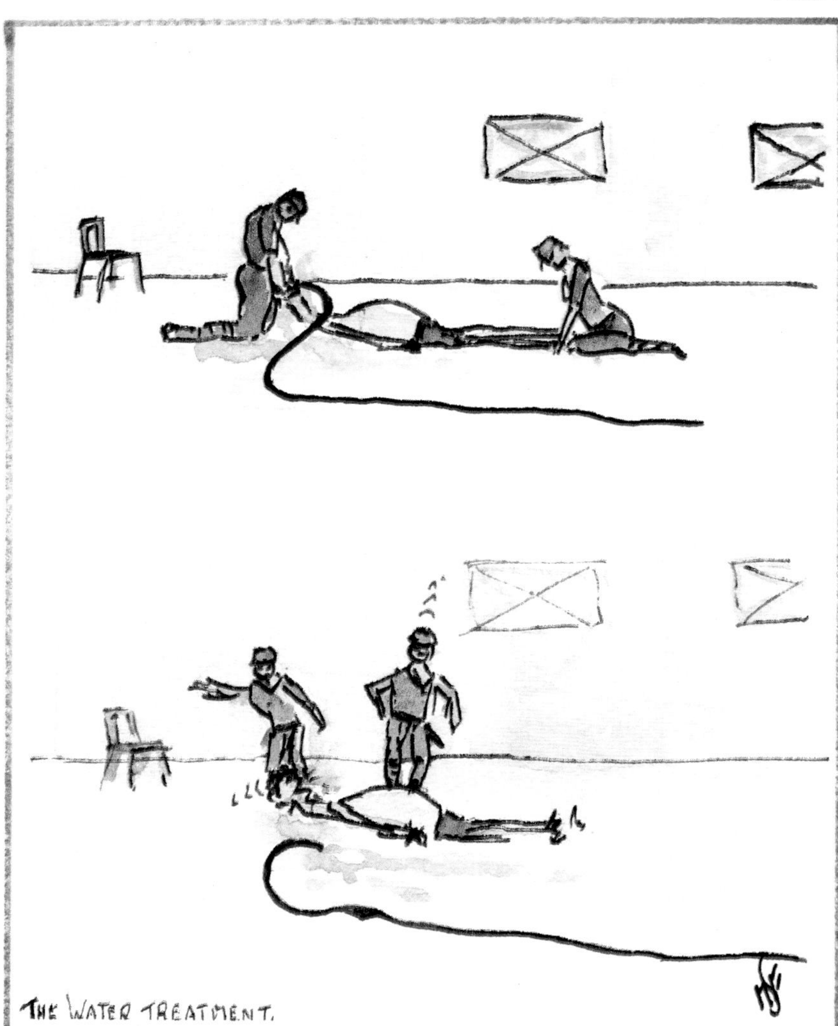

THE WATER TREATMENT.
THE VICTIM'S WRISTS AND ANKLES ARE BOUND WITH BARBED WIRE.
WATER IS FORCED INTO HIS STOMACH THROUGH A HOSE.
WHEN STOMACH IS PAINFULLY EXTENDED, JAPANESE JUMPS ON STOMACH,
OTHER JAP KICKS VICTIM'S HEAD.

Plate 7

AMUSEMENT FOR JAPANESE GUARDS
DURING HALF HOUR REST PERIOD

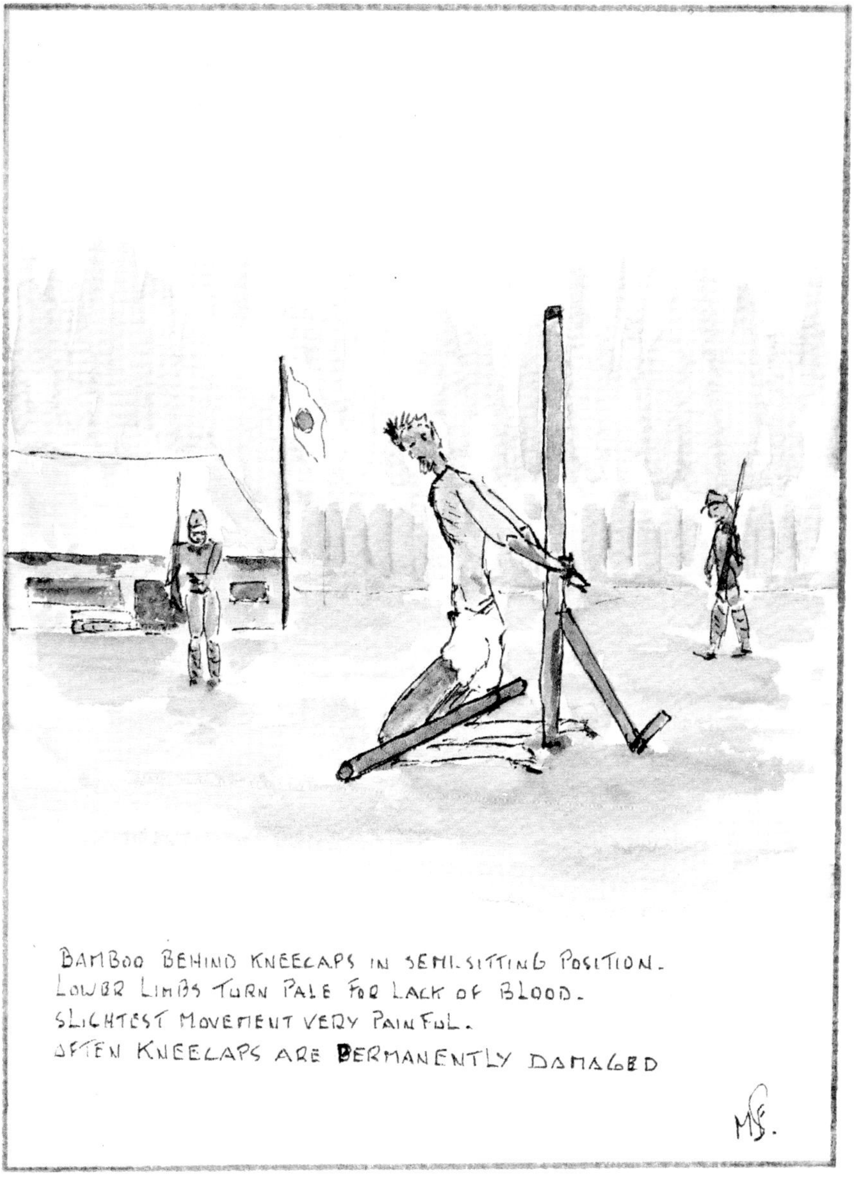

BAMBOO BEHIND KNEECAPS IN SEMI-SITTING POSITION.
LOWER LIMBS TURN PALE FOR LACK OF BLOOD.
SLIGHTEST MOVEMENT VERY PAINFUL.
OFTEN KNEECAPS ARE PERMANENTLY DAMAGED

Plate 9

P.O.W.s. PILE DRIVING FOUNDATION FOR BRIDGE OVER THE RIVER KWAE.
WORKING FROM DAWN TILL DUSK. STANDING HIP DEEP IN FAST FLOWING RIVER.

Plate 11

UNLOADING 50 K.G. RICE SACKS
FOR JAPANESE UPHILL, DURING
MONSOON. BAMBOO SHOOTS IN MUD,
PENETRATE BARE FEET OF P.O.W.S.
CAUSING DREADED TROPICAL ULCERS.
MB.

Plate 13

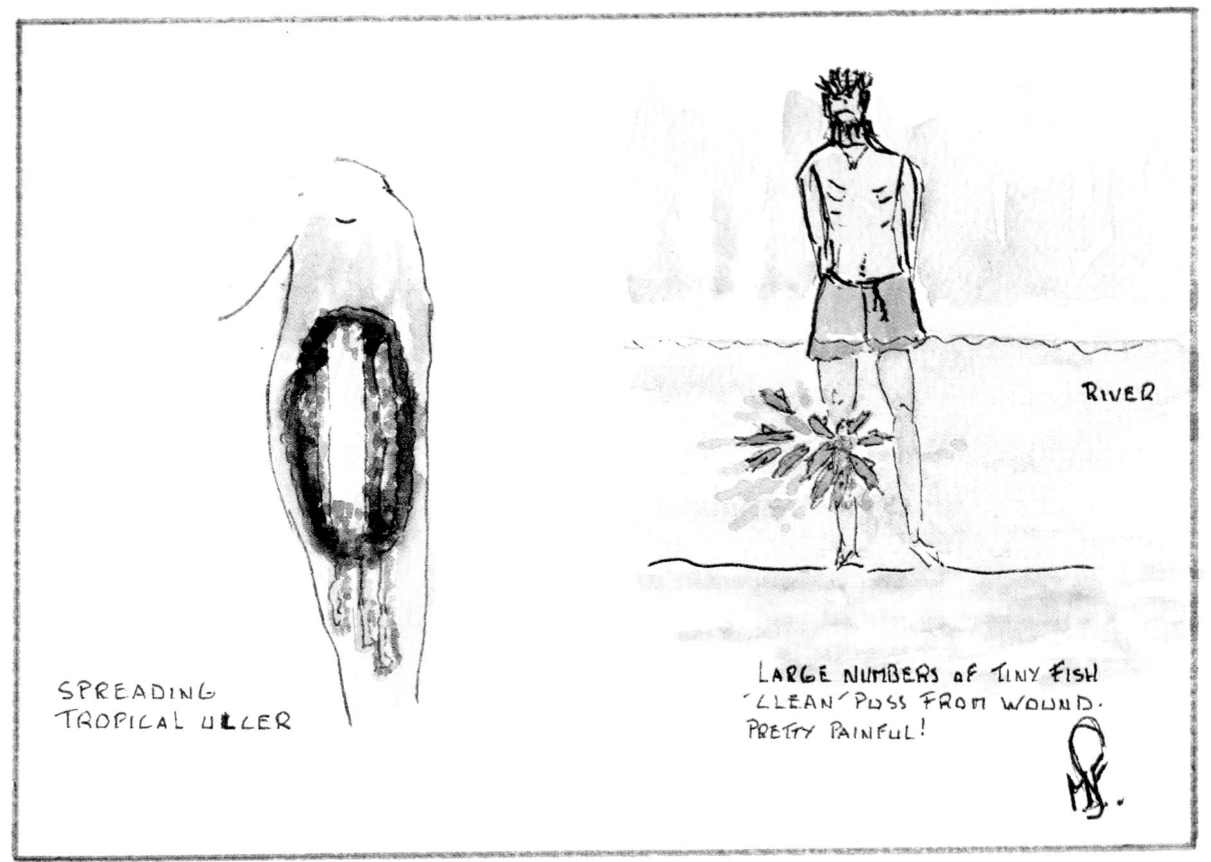
SPREADING
TROPICAL ULCER
RIVER
LARGE NUMBERS OF TINY FISH
'CLEAN' PUSS FROM WOUND.
PRETTY PAINFUL!

-CHOLERA-

Plate 15

JAPANESE 'NURSES'
RIVER
THIN BAMBOO STICK
FOR SHOWING EXCITEMENT AFTER LEWD GESTURES BY JAPANESE 'NURSES'

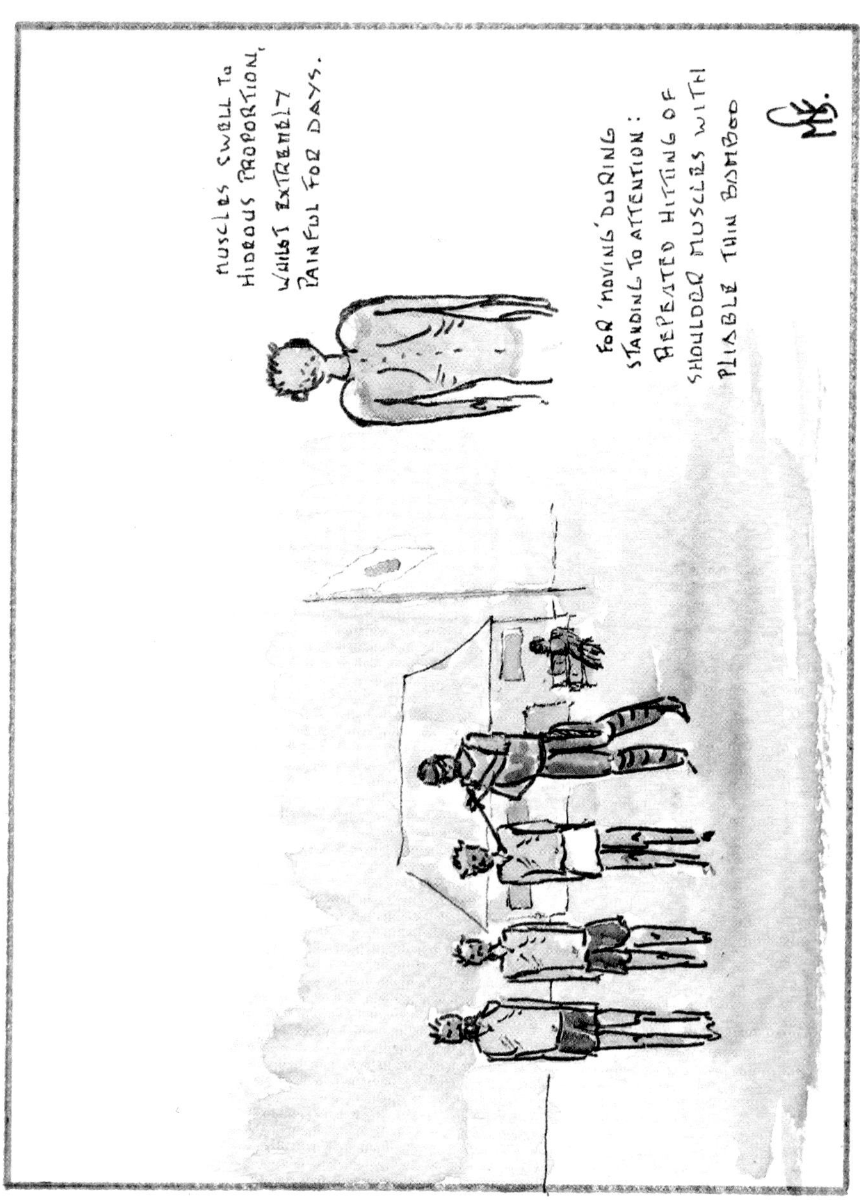
MUSCLES SWELL TO
HIDEOUS PROPORTION,
WHILST EXTREMELY
PAINFUL FOR DAYS.
FOR 'MOVING' DURING
STANDING TO ATTENTION :
REPEATED HITTING OF
SHOULDER MUSCLES WITH
PLIABLE THIN BAMBOO

Plate 17

EARLY MORNING 18TH. AUGUST 1945
JAPS LEFT JUNGLE CAMP DURING NIGHT.
JAPS SURRENDERED ON 15TH AUGUST.
FREEDOM WAS THREE DAYS LATE.

Plate 19

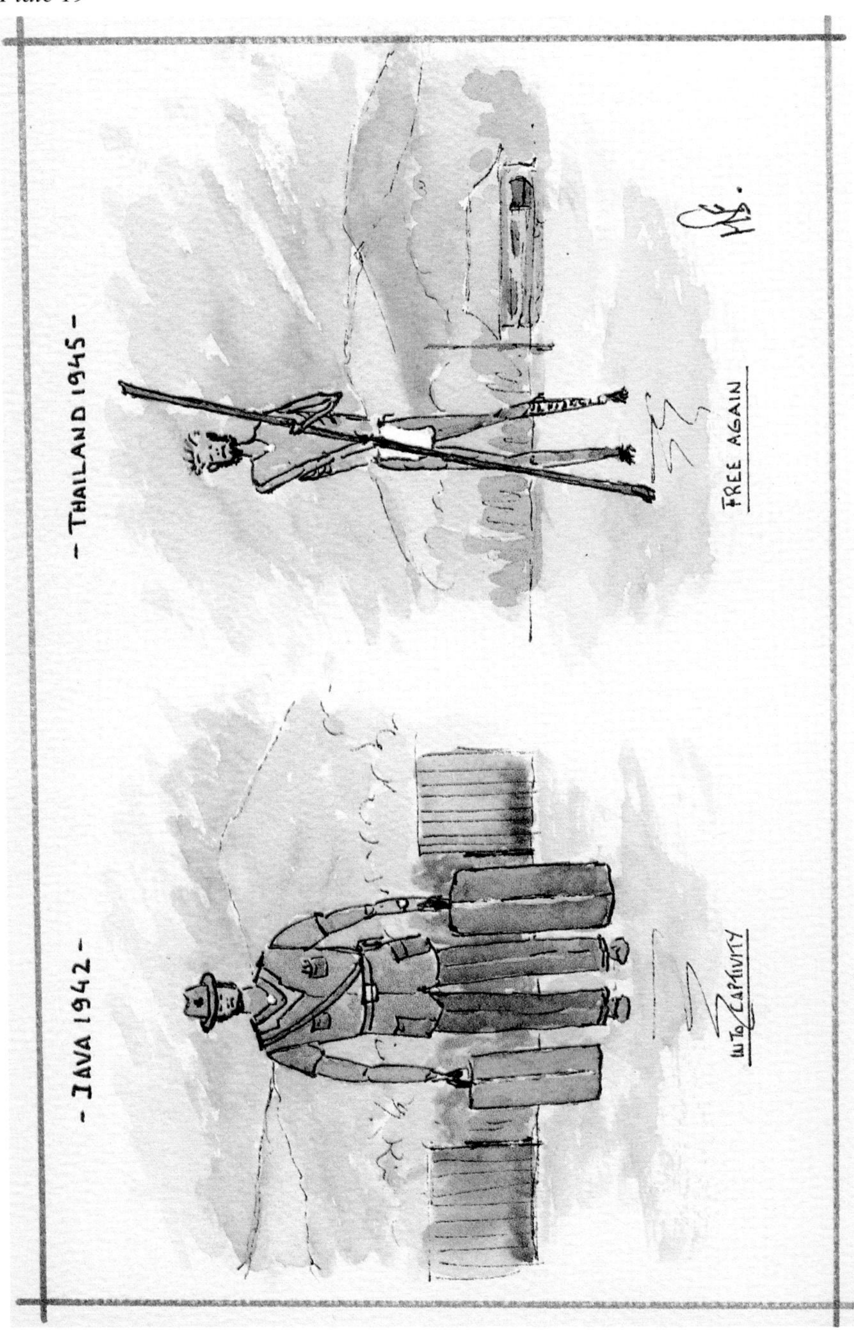

Plate 20

Kwai Bridge after the R.A.F. bombing raid of 1945

Plate 21

MB.

FAILED ESCAPE BID

16 AUGUST 1945

(ONE DAY AFTER JAPANESE SURRENDER)

IN HONOURED REMEMBRANCE OF THE FORTITUDE AND SACRIFICE OF THAT VALIANT COMPANY WHO PERISHED WHILE BUILDING THE RAILWAY FROM THAILAND TO BURMA DURING THEIR LONG CAPTIVITY
THOSE WHO HAVE NO KNOWN GRAVE ARE COMMEMORATED BY NAME AT RANGOON SINGAPORE AND HONG KONG AND THEIR COMRADES REST IN THE THREE WAR CEMETERIES OF KANCHANABURI CHUNGKAI AND THANBYUZAYAT
I will make you a name and a praise among all people of the earth when I turn back your captivity before your eyes, saith the LORD

Visit to Kanchanaburi Cemetery in 1983

"SMILES"

A day in the life of a Japanese P.O.W.
on the Railroad of Death
by
Fred Seiker

It was the year 1944. Somewhere near the Three Pagoda Pass on the Thai-Burma border. They had force marched us from sunrise to sunset for two days, "us" being prisoners of war, "they" being two Japanese soldiers. The group consisted of Dutch and British POWs.

We were pronounced "fit" by a Japanese medical person with the rank of private, who assured us that we were going for a "short walk, good camp". Experience told us that this meant "long walk, no camp".

Ahead of the column strode the Japanese sergeant, our pathfinder and pace setter. At the rear a disgruntled Japanese private slouched along, prodding stragglers with a bayonet ridiculously large for the size of the soldier.

The jungle was oppressively hot, humid and dense. We carried our rations, cooking utensils (discarded oil cans) and tools on three makeshift carriers. The carriers were made up of old rice sacks and bamboo poles, a kind of stretcher. Each stretcher was carried by a team of four men. Those with ulcerated legs were not required to be pack mules. This was not a Japanese gesture. It was our decision, after lengthy arguments and several face slapping sessions from the sergeant.

One team was already carrying a man who had collapsed with dysentery. The two remaining teams now had to carry the additional load of the stretcher occupied by the sick man. The sergeant would not allow us to make up a fourth stretcher, because he had already given us a concession with regard to the men with ulcerated legs!

We had not drunk a sip of water all day. Our bodies were dried out, our throats were hoarse, our tongues felt like leather strips in our mouths. We were giddy from exhaustion and most of us suffered stomach cramp. The familiar gibbon calls could no longer be heard. It meant there was no fresh water for miles around.

We made camp at dusk in a clearing close to a muddy pool, alive with insects. Several thrust their faces into the murky water, drinking greedily. Moves to stop them were met with violent objections. Most likely we would bury some of them, later. The Japs grinned!

Fires were lit for boiling the pool water and cooking the maggot infested rice.

A portion of this and a small piece of dried fish was our meal for the day, washed down with boiled brown pool water.

Our bodies ached and our minds were numb as we crouched around the fires, which were kept burning to keep wild animals at bay. No one spoke. What was there to talk about? Each man was cocooned within his own thoughts. They were a comfort, your own thoughts. The night was black now. The jungle canopy had closed in over us.

I realised that further marching the following day would decimate our numbers. Was that the plan perhaps? A chill ran down my spine. For the first time in my life I knew total misery. I felt alone and very frightened.

Then I became aware of a voice mingling with the many sounds of the night jungle. At first softly, haltingly, then louder, more certain, singing "Ave Maria" in a clear tenor voice. The jungle sounds around us subsided one by one as if the night creatures were also listening.

The voice was now singing jubilantly and triumphantly. It was a moment of awe and wonder. The voice filled our hearts and minds as it rose into the silent blackness above us. I knew then that this magic moment would sustain me in whatever situation I would find myself in the future.

Faces lifted, tears glistening in the fire's glow. Men struggled to their feet, some helped by their comrades. It seemed an impulsive gesture of defiance, as if to say, "We cannot be beaten". Were they feeling the same as I did? Were they also ashamed of their earlier misgivings?

I believed they were. A glow of pride rose within me. A pride of belonging. Also a feeling of victory. Victory of the human spirit over adversity.

Both Japanese soldiers eyed us with bewilderment and suspicion, rifles at the ready. Their eyes darted around the group of quiet men. Men with haggard faces, damp rags hanging from their bones. We were no threat to their wellbeing, yet their eyes showed fear. Fear of something they could not understand. I felt pity for them, then.

As the voice softly remingled with the returning jungle sounds, the Japanese soldier suddenly snapped, shouting "kurra, kurra", threatening everyone in sight with the glistening, menacing bayonet.

As he approached me I smiled. It sent him into a rage. After all, how do you fight a smile? The rifle butt thudded into my body, sending me crashing to the ground *(Plate 23)*. I looked up into his face, now grinning, fury spent, the ridiculously large bayonet aimed at my throat! After a short while the Jap ambled away, kicking the ground as he went, mumbling to himself.

My mates hauled me back onto my feet. Their eyes tearful with suppressed anger. I realised then that my chest was throbbing with pain. "No sense of humour, these bastards," someone murmured. I smiled. How right he was.

Plate 23

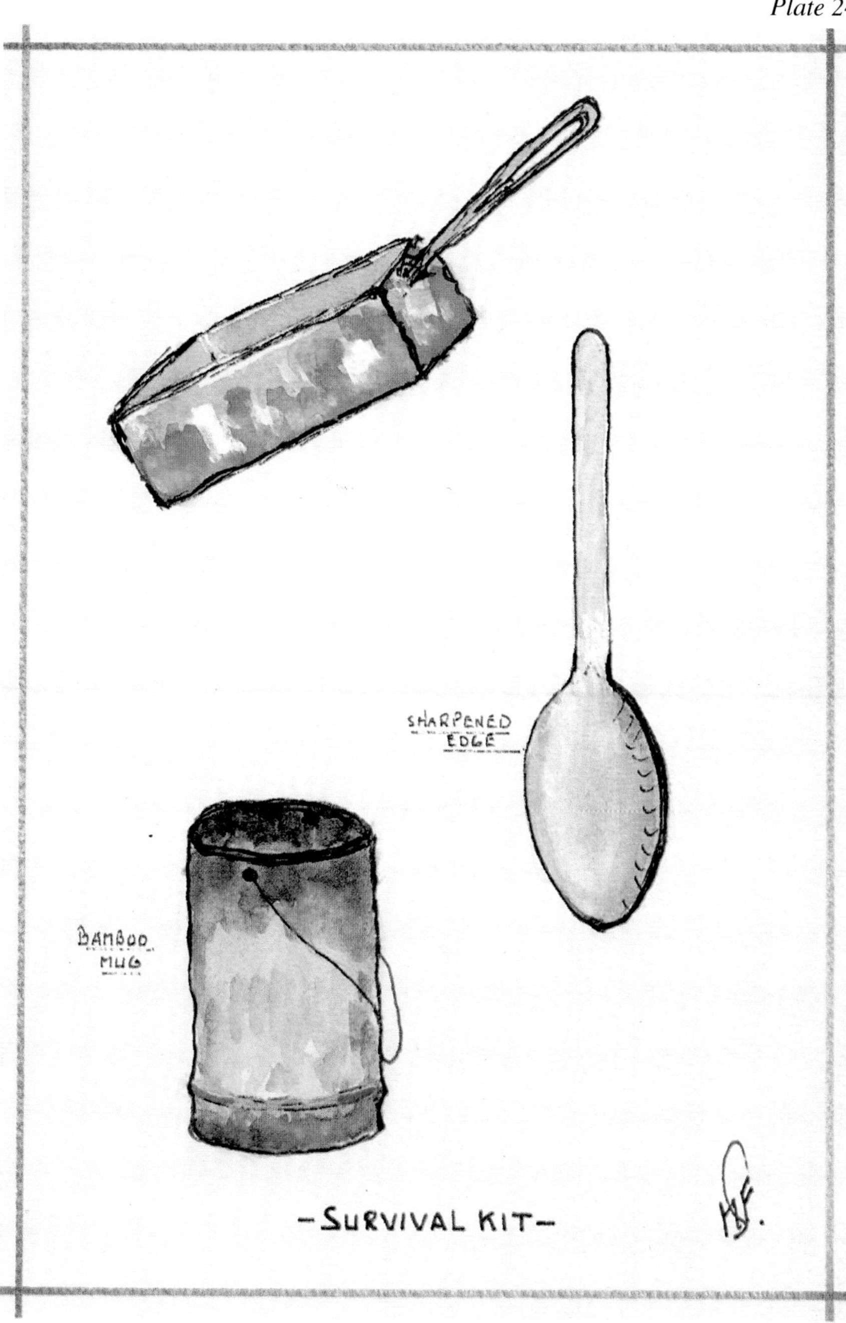
SHARPENED EDGE
BAMBOO MUG
-SURVIVAL KIT-

Plate 25

Restored Kwai Bridge

Revisiting the Kwai Bridge in 1983

NOTES TO THE PLATES

Plate 1 The reason for this man's nickname is obvious. A large number of Koreans volunteered into the Imperial Japanese Army. Their duties were mainly confined to guarding POW camps along the railway. This they did with great zeal. Their sadistic brutalities were feared by all POWs. Horseface was one of the worst. The Koreans were obsessed with the idea that they must prove to their masters their total obedience. This they did with a vengeance.

Plate 2 Fit parade. It was called thus because the word 'sick' does not appear in Japanese POW philosophy. Every morning the sick bays would be raided by a Jap, with much shouting and bashing. The standing, the kneeling and the lying down were lined up outside their huts. A Jap, usually of minor rank, would decide who was fit for work. The attending POW camp medic usually bore the brunt of any beatings because of objections to the brutal inhuman decisions by the Jap. As a rule, those who could stand unaided were sent to the railway site for work, often returning at night on a makeshift stretcher, dead.

Plate 3 Another common torture. The author on this occasion pinched a tin of fruit from the Japanese cookhouse and was caught by a Jap guard. It was part of the Red Cross consignments for the POWṣ which never reached the prisoners, but were always confiscated by the Japs for their own use. The victim is tied to a tree in view of the Jap guard house. A bucket of fresh water is placed in front of him and he is then left for a period of about 48 hours. A period which usually suffices for the victim to collapse. Anyone trying to approach him suffers the same treatment. A tricky situation arises the next day, when the Japs insist that he turns out for work on the railway.

Plate 4 Thumbs suspension. Another favourite for minor offences. Sometimes this was used for failing to bow to a guard. Very often the guard in question was hiding in a dark place after sun down, i.e. he could not be seen. After passing the guard he would jump out and butt you with his rifle and you were marched off to the guard house where you were beaten. A tree close to the guard house was the next venue, where you were suspended by your thumbs, with your toes just touching the ground. It caused great pain in arms and lower leg muscles.

Plate 5 This torture was also a punishment for minor misdeeds such as forgetting to bow to a passing guard. Triangular sections of wood were nailed to a tea chest or similar object. The victim was then forced onto the timbers with his feet just overhanging the edge of the chest. His knees and shinbones would be resting on the sharp timbers. A boulder of considerable weight would be placed into his cradled arms, increasing the downward weight onto the knees and shinbones. A period of three to four hours was usually the limit of endurance, after which the Japs allowed the victim to be lifted off the timbers. Damage to kneecaps was the usual longterm result.

Plate 6 Water treatment. This was a special of the Kempitai (Japanese Military Police). It was usually used to obtain a 'confession'. Water would be forced into the victims stomach as the sketch portrays. The pain from the stomach extension alone was extreme. Jumping up and down on the victim's swollen stomach bears no description. As an addition the victim's head would be kicked about, adding to the enjoyment of the torturers. Many 'confessed' in order to escape more torture. That in itself caused further punishment.

Plate 7 Boulder lifting. This was very popular with the Jap guards as a means of amusement, not always as a result of a misdeed. It was usually carried out at random during rest periods. A P.O.W. would be picked out and told to stand to attention. A heavy boulder would be placed into his cradled arms whilst standing to attention. The Japs would then either prod his back with a bayonet or kick his legs from behind. The resulting stumble always caused great hilarity from the Japs and immense restraint from the P.O.W's not to retaliate.

Plate 8 Bamboo behind knee-caps. A punishment for minor misdeeds. It caused the lower legs to be starved of blood and the knee caps to be put under immense stress, with possible problems in later life.

Plate 9 Knight of Bushido. Beheadings of POWs were carried out for various reasons. It was always the subject of a Japanese stage show. The entire camp would be forced to witness these executions and were always under threat of armed guards. Stealing so-called Japanese property, insulting a Jap officer or trying to escape were sufficient reason for this barbarity to be carried out. Beheadings of POWs were often carried out as a method of practising the 'art' of decapitating. Witnesses have described the horror when the first sword stroke is not decisive! The Bushido code contains among other accolades that a Bushido must be kind and benevolent to the weak and innocent.

Plate 10 Pile driving for the Kwai river bridge. Work was carried out from early morning to late evening. Every phase of this operation was executed by manpower only. A Japanese guard would stand on the embankment and dictate through a loudhailer the rhythm of the 'pull' and 'release' operations. POWs were standing waist deep in water all day. The counting from the riverbank was relentless whatever the problems. Tree trunks and other debris were a constant hazard. With a fast flowing river they caused many accidents, sometimes fatal, to the amusement of the guards.

Plate 11 Unloading of rice sacks. In itself not a torture. But if carried out by undernourished and diseased bodies it becomes an almost impossible task. Add to this the monsoon season and a muddy, slippery hill with treacherous bamboo spikes hidden in the mud, then this work turns into a hell on earth. Anyone who had the misfortune to tumble with a 50 kg load on his back was immediately set upon by a guard beating him with rifle butt or heavy stick.

Plate 12 This was the main activity of most POWs, the building of the rail embankment. It was a dawn to dusk task carried out with unerring brutality and beatings from the Japs, because it was their method of trying to achieve more and more output from the slaveworkers. Each day the workforce was divided into sections. Each section was given an identical task to fulfil for the day, irrespective of the ground condition, ie some sections were easier to work than others. Protests as to the impossibility of the given task resulted in a thorough beating by one or more guards. If by chance one section appeared to fulfil the requirement for the day, more was added to all sections the following day. It was a no win situation at all times. Soil was carried by one person in a basket or in makeshift stretchers carried by two people.

Plate 13 Tropical ulcer. The most dreaded of all sores. The slightest scratch could start this awful rotting disease. Bamboo wounds usually turned into a spreading ulcer. There were of course no medicines of any kind available for the P.O.W's, the only way to keep wounds reasonably clean was to scrape them with a sharpened spoon. This was usually done by holding the victim down by his arms and feet, whilst medical personnel carried out the gruesome task of scraping the wound. Many leg amputations were carried out as a result of tropical ulcers.

Plate 14 Cholera epidemic. An experience of mind numbing proportion. A situation where death becomes acceptable as a routine. Cholera can kill within 24 hours, from reasonable health to certain death. The Japs were terrified of this mass killer. In this particular case they barricaded the entry of the camp and relocated themselves about two miles away and did not return until their own medical staff declared the camp safe. For various reasons we were not allowed to bury our dead in the usual pits but were ordered to incinerate the bodies within the confines of the camp. This was an ongoing operation, day and night. Words cannot describe the horror of the dying and the living.

Plate 15 Nurses in river incident. This must count among the most loathsome of tortures a human being could contrive. A P.O.W. would be ordered into the river where Japanese 'nurses' were bathing in the nude. He would be forced to wash their back watched by his fellow P.O.W.'s. He would be called back to the river bank upon which the 'nurses' would make lewd gestures. If the P.O.W. showed even the slightest sign of sexual excitement the guard would hit his penis with a slender pliable bamboo. The extreme pain and mental humiliation for the P.O.W. was complete. It is understood that some P.O.W.'s suffered mental anguish from this torture, long after their release.

Plate 16 Shoulder tapping. This was very popular among some of the Korean guards. The victim stood to attention whilst the guard kept hitting his shoulder muscles. At first the pain was bearable then the pain would almost cease. All the time the guard was hitting your shoulders. Then you realised that the shoulder muscles were swelling to almost your earlobes. The victim would then have to stand to attention for a further hour or so, before being allowed to stand down. After a while the pain returned with vengeance. This could last for up to three days, before the swelling went down.

Plate 17 This is not a torture subject as such. The sleeping space allowed per person was about two feet. The bed base consisted of split bamboos tied together with cut and dried bamboo leaves (atap) and secured to a framework of bamboo poles. The bamboo always became infested with lice and bugs. You could tell the lice from the bugs because the lice were white in colour, whilst the bugs were brownish-red depending on how much human blood they had consumed. The lice were a constant menace during the monsoon season because there was no heat from the sun to kill them. The bugs were very much a case of catch them whilst and when you can.

Plate 18 Freedom. This event took place deep into the Thai jungle not far from the Three Pagodas Pass. One early morning on August 18, 1945 the author went to the latrine without being challenged and slapped by a guard. The silence was eerie. He collected his mate and together they crept towards the Jap guardhouse. There were no Japs in sight. At first he expected a trap. Not so, they had gone! So had their kitchen, stores transport etc. The lot. It took them a day or two to realise that this was for real. A native confirmed that the Japs had gone. They were free men once again.

Plate 19 Java 1942. The author walks into a Japanese POW camp in Bandung, Java. Totally ignorant and utterly naive about what was to follow. Civilisation as known ceased immediately. To be turned into a subservient 'nothing' within minutes is impossible to describe. But such is the human spirit, that the majority of Japanese POWs did survive. Just. 18th August 1945, somewhere near the Three Pagodas Pass in Thailand. Emaciated, hungry, weak and sick but happy. Freedom AT LAST.

Plate 20 RAF bombing of the River Kwai bridge in 1945. It knocked out two sections of this major strategic bridge, crippling the Jap supply lines. The two destroyed sections were replaced after the war. The Thai Railway now operates a diesel train service, not further than Nam Tok. The remainder of the entire railway has been reclaimed by the jungle. Many Allied POWs lie in unmarked graves along the rail track, thousands of miles from their respective homelands. What utter, utter waste of human life.

Plate 21 Japan surrendered to the Allies on 15th August 1945. The POW depicted made an escape bid on the 16th August. It was a foolish thing to even contemplate. There was virgin jungle all around us. Local tribesmen were not always trustworthy, as the victim was soon to discover. He was returned to the camp, hands tied behind his back, by a group of local tribesmen. It is believed that the Japs paid handsomely for such betrayal. This victim was bayonetted to death only hours after his recapture. The tragedy of the story is that the war had officially ended one day previously. Whether the Japs knew was never established.

Plate 24 Survival kit. Towards the end of the war these were the only possessions most POWs working on the railway were concerned about. They were their lifeline. The food tin was the prime item. It served all basic requirements for sustaining human life. The metal spoon was a luxury, because one side could be sharpened to serve as a cutting implement. If however a Jap spotted it the spoon was taken away and the owner repeatedly beaten. No POW was allowed to have in his possession anything with a sharp edge. The safest thing was to shape a spoon from bamboo which could also be replaced quite easily. The bamboo mug was also easily obtainable and could be fashioned to different sizes. It was however essential that any bamboo implement used for drinking or eating was thoroughly singed until black, because bamboo slivers, however small, are potential killers if trapped in the human digestive system.

Plates 25 & 26 Revisiting the Kwai bridge. The author and his wife visited the Kanchanabury cemetery (Thailand) and the Kwai bridge in 1983. It was a very emotional and stressful experience. More so, since that day a large contingent of Japanese tourists arrived, many of them of similar age to that of the author. They strutted about explaining things to their compatriots, obviously proud of their achievements of years ago. They posed for photographs beside a monument dedicated to the fallen on the railway.

THE
THAI-BURMA RAILWAY
AND BEYOND

FORGIVE? The dead cannot judge

FORGET? The dead are for ever

I became a POW of the Japanese in Bandoeng, Java, soon after the Japanese occupied the island. I walked into the POW camp with two suitcases filled with all manner of food. The cases were immediately ripped from my grasp. My objections to this robbery were rejected by Japanese fists slamming into my face and a rifle butt sending me crashing to the ground. A Japanese officer explained to me in English that I was now a POW of the Imperial Japanese Army and as such had no rights whatever. They then proceeded to remove my personal belongings, watch, fotographs, money etc. The humiliation was complete. In just minutes I ceased to be a person. I believe to this day that they considered a worm in the earth of greater value than a POW.

I was shown my temporary quarters, which consisted of the veranda of an abandoned bungalow, which I shared with two other POWs. The veranda was open to the elements, wet and draughty at times. We soon organised ourselves in some kind of routine and waited for things to develop. Which they did!

One late afternoon the entire camp was ordered on parade. We were confronted with the spectacle of three sailors, each tied to a wooden pole. A Japanese officer explained that these three chaps had escaped from the camp, but were soon caught and were now waiting to be executed. A rumble rippled through the assembled POWs. It was a tense moment, but the cocked machine guns placed around the parade ground, trained on us, soon calmed things down. The sailors were executed by bayonet thrusts in the throat, the stomach and lower abdomen. Their death was designed to be painful and slow. A warning to future escapees! It also became clear to us what kind of thugs we were dealing with.

One evening it was announced that we would be taken to another place, where we would be put to work on building a railroad. Those who followed orders would be well treated, others would receive harsh but fair treatment.

Convoys of lorries took us to Tandjong Priok, the port of Batavia, now Djakarta. We were herded onto a shabby old rust bucket and driven into the holds of the ....Maru. To describe the scene is one of those occasions when even an imaginative mind fails to grasp the horror of it all. We were stacked-and I mean stacked-onto elevated platforms within the holds of the vessel. The horizontal space per man was just enough to turn over without landing on your neighbour. Vertical space was not quite enough to sit up. A dim light at the end of each row of bodies was the only light that could be seen. Each hold had one single opening at the top for ventilation. At each opening stood a Japanese guard, who was in total command of who was allowed on deck for natural functions. If he decided not to allow you on deck, you were confronted with a huge menacing bayonet. A hasty retreat back into hell followed. The natural function then took place in the hold. The first dysentery cases began to appear.

The trip to Singapore took several days. Our misery and humiliation at that time was total. On arrival in Singapore we were transported to Changi Jail. Time at Changi was not too bad. The Japs left us alone and we ran our own affairs.

Food was inadequate, but little extra's could be obtained through various obscure channels.

The time had come when we were transported to Thailand. We found ourselves packed into steel railway trucks, intended for transportation of cattle or rice. I shall not describe our journey which took several days. Various books on the subject have been published, describing this hell on wheels in detail. We eventually arrived at a place called Kanchanabury, where we were housed in a long bamboo hut. The floor consisted of mud, the sleeping platforms were constructed of bamboo slats, the allocated space per man was about two feet and the roof in many places open to the sky. This was to be our home for some time to come. It soon became evident that the question of camp and personal hygiene were crucial to one's survival.

I wish to mention something which is usually avoided in the many books published about this episode. The large base camps in the south of Thailand held thousands of men from various countries, each with their own distinctive way of life. The British had their community spirit, the Aussies their egalitarian attitude, the Dutch their individualism, the Americans were not in evidence at that time. It should therefore not be too surprising to hear that during the days of early captivity, ugly scenes took place among the POWs. Fist fights were the order of the day, until we realised that the Japs took great delight in our squabbles. The camp atmosphere changed for the better, which also made us realise that we depended upon each other in times ahead.

Our group was soon put to work on the foundations for the Kwai bridge at Tamarkan. We were detailed to drive wooden piles into the river bed for the foundations of the concrete bridge supports. The usual mechanical construction machinery for this type of work was totally absent. Several triangular wooden pole structures were erected which carried a pulley at the top. A stout rope was fed over the pulley. One end of the rope carried a heavy steel ram; the other end was splayed into several leaders, which in turn were held by POWs standing in the river bed. Straight tree trunks were obtained from the surrounding forest, transported to the bridge site by elephants or floated from upcountry downstream, where a Jap decided which ones were to be used for piling. The tree trunks were hauled into position beneath the ram and pile driving began. On the command of a guard standing on the riverbank shouting through a megaphone the required rhythm at which HE decided that piling should take place.

You pulled in unison, you let go in unison. 'Ichi, ni,san, shi, ichi, ni, san, shi', on and on and on. Hour after hour after hour. Day in, day out. From dawn to dusk, unrelenting. On returning to camp at night it was difficult to raise the spoon to eat the slop issued to us. Your arms protested in pain, often preventing you from snatching some precious sleep. And yet, come dawn you repeated the misery of the previous day. I often wondered about the miracle of the human body and mind. Believe me, it is quite awesome.

I was fortunate in that I was engaged in the piling operation for only a short while. Our group was taken up-country to begin work on the rail embankment. This meant we were to occupy smaller camps, run by Japanese non-commissioned officers. These thugs were usually power drunk, sadistic, evil individuals.

Building embankments consisted of carrying earth from alongside the track to the top of the ever growing embankment. You carried a basket from the digging area to the top of the embankment, emptied it and down again to be filled for your next trip up the hill. Simple really. But in reality this job was far from easy. The slopes of the embankments consisted of loose earth, clambering to the top was a case of sliding and slithering with a weight of earth in attendance. This proved to be very tiring on thigh muscles and painful, often resulting in crippling cramp. You just had to stop, you could not move. Whenever this occurred the guards were on you with their heavy sticks and beat the living daylight out of you. Somehow, you got going again, if only to escape the blows. Also, the soil alongside the track varied considerably, affecting the volume of earth an individual was able to move during a day. At the start of each day, a guard would decide the total volume of earth to be dug out that day. By the nature of things, some finished earlier than others. The volume the following day was fixed by the fastest time obtained the previous day, thereby increasing the total workload of the entire team. It was a truly 'no win' situation. If a group of the team was running late, everyone worked on until the stipulated volume for that day was achieved. This meant that the guards also had to stay behind. They relieved their anger and frustration by random beatings of the POWs, sometimes resulting in serious injury to the POWs.

On arriving back at the camp a head count was carried out by the guards. The number of POWs counted then, were expected to turn up for work on the railway the following morning, ignoring those who were too ill for work because of the beating they had received or were seriously ill.

It was a never changing scenario. The orderly who presented the guard with his sick list was always without fail beaten up in a show of Japanese rage. The poor sick individuals were then dragged from the so called hospital and forced to work on the railway. Sometimes they returned to the camp that night, carried on a sack stretcher, dead! These were by no means isolated incidents, they occurred on a daily basis all along the rail track.

As we know, numerous individuals have been praised and honoured for their humanitarian work in the base camps, often enduring horrendous treatment from the Japanese camp commanders for refusing to carry out their stupid orders. These individuals deserve our admiration and deepest respect.

On the other hand, the orderly in the jungle camp carried out his work with steadfast dedication. He protected his charges with unstinting valour, day in, day out, often moving with great pain in his body from the beatings he received. He knew for certain that every time he tried to protect his mates, he would receive a merciless beating.

He never flinched, although he did not know whether he would be able to walk away from the next beating. That, to me is heroism of the highest order. Where are these men now? I do not recall seeing their names in the honours lists.

I have been intrigued by ex-POWs who readily remember the names of the guards and all the camps they occupied. Perhaps it is because I was never long enough in a particular camp to become familiar with their names. Although, I must confess that the names of the guards never did have much significance for me. However, there is always the exception and that is 'Horseface'. The reason for this nickname becomes obvious when one looks at the sketch of his face depicted in this book. He was a Korean guard of the worst type. The Korean guards were sent to the smaller camps in which I so often found myself. This thug is the only one I would love to meet again on my own ground, even today.

He was the original pervert and sadist. His main enjoyment consisted of loitering at the tail end of a column of POWs returning from a day's slavery on the railway and prodding any stragglers with his bayonet, the point of which he had honed to a razor sharp edge. It never caused serious damage, but it always drew a trickle of blood. On spotting the blood he would grunt with pleasure, face distorted in ecstasy. He would then select his next victim.

I would also like to demonstrate the crazy philosophy of these creatures. It refers to what I call the kitchen incident. In one camp in the North of Thailand, it occurred that it was my turn to raid the Jap cookhouse in the hope of finding something edible. It was known to us that the Japs had confiscated a consignment of Red Cross parcels, which was their usual procedure. I was able to nick a tin of fruit. On my way back to my eagerly waiting mates, I was suddenly confronted with a glistening bayonet followed by a kick in the groin. I was terrified. I was marched to the Japanese guard house with the bayonet in close attendance. The ritual beating began. Several of the guards pounced on me at the same time. When eventually the sergeant in charge of the camp appeared, he ordered them to stop. I could not have been a pretty sight, I certainly did not feel like one. The sergeant drew his sword and pointed it at my neck, grinning. He addressed me in broken English, from which I understood that stealing from the Imperial Japanese Army was a serious crime against the Emperor and would be punished by chopping my head off. At some point I managed to explain to him that I could not possibly be a thief by taking something that was mine in the first place. He did not appreciate the logic of my defence and he ordered that I be taken to the punishment tree some ten yards in front of the guard house. I had watched many a comrade undergo the sergeant's favourite punishment and realised that it was now my turn. I was propped against the tree, my arms pulled back and tied at the wrists behind the tree trunk. My feet were tied together and secured to the tree trunk. After a few more punches in the face, they left me alone. The pain that lashes your body after a while I must leave to the reader's imagination. When morning broke they placed a wooden bucket filled to the brim with water in front of me. A sophisticated torture if ever there was one. Parade was called for the usual head count prior to work on the railway.

The sergeant then explained to the assembled POWs that this was the punishment for stealing from the Imperial Japanese Army and that I would be executed later on that day. The terror of it was, that you never knew whether it was an idle threat or an official announcement. I regained consciousness in the so called 'hospital', with the orderly trying to pour water into my mouth. I never did find out why I was caught, though there was a suspicion. These things did happen now and then. A short while later I was back on the railway.

CHOLERA! Once you have lived through a cholera epidemic in a Japanese POW camp, you do not have to be afraid of ever finding yourself in hell. You have endured the worst scenario hell can produce.

Overnight the huts were filled with the dead and the dying. The guards were terrified of this disease and hastily retreated to a safe distance away from the camp after barricading the entrance to the camp with Xshaped barricades and rolls of razor wire.

We were instructed to incinerate our dead, not to bury them. Cholera strikes swiftly, without warning. It is terminal in the absence of medication. Our medic's kit did not contain even an aspirin tablet. Combined with the emaciated state we were in, the onslaught was terrifying. You could be O.K. in the morning and dead in the evening the same day. Once dehydration set in, your place on the pyre was assured.

I was one of a team attending the funeral pyre for a while and depositing the bodies of my friends into the flames. This was a round the clock operation. It was macabre and frightening at first. A corpse would suddenly sit up amidst the flames, or an arm or a leg would extend jerkily. But even this horror soon became a routine job.

On the subject of acceptance of death, I recall a typical incident. One day, after a long work period on the railway, a mate next to me laid down for the night's rest. Before falling asleep he turned to me and said: "I feel lousy mate and very tired." The next morning I shook him gently to wake him for the morning parade. He did not wake up. He was dead. Died during the night. Quietly. The orderlies came and took him away. Another identity tag into the rusty metal tin! At some time during the day, someone would say: "Where is old Tony"? The reply was: "He's had it, packed up last night". A voice would mutter: "Lucky bastard, he's out of it". There never was intended disrespect. Death had become an accepted part of our existence on the Railway of Death.

The cholera outbreak lasted for several horrendous days. It took away many of my friends. I do not recall the total death toll. It became evident after the war, that some native labour camps were entirely wiped out because of cholera.

The railway was completed on October 17, 1943, at Konkuita in Thailand, not far from the Three Pagodas Pass. I shall not enter into the statistics or technical data or the final death toll of the various countries involved in building the Thai-Burma Railway; these have been extensively reported elsewhere.

When the railway was completed, teams of workers were formed by the Japanese, moving up and down the track repairing and maintaining bridges, tracks, embankments etc. I was one of a group sent to Northern Thailand and into Burma , to dig caves into the hill sides. These caves were used by the Japanese for ammunition storage. The caves were connected to the railway by heavily camouflaged tracks, so they could not be spotted from the air. We often considered the risk we represented to the Japanese because of our knowledge of the location of these caves. It seemed not to bother them. Later we were ordered to dig 'tanktraps' in close proximity to our camp. Tanktraps in the middle of virgin jungle asked ourselves. These tanktraps were of considerable length and width. Then someone offered the thought that these tanktraps looked remarkably like mass graves. I have no personal knowledge of this, but it would appear that later found evidence proved the Jap's intent to massacre our group in the tanktraps and bulldoze earth over the remains. We would have disappeared for all time.

Then HIROSHIMA happened. On the 18th of August 1945 at dawn I went on my usual trip to the latrines, expecting the ritual early morning bashing from a guard for either not spotting him in time to bow, or bowing to an empty space, whilst he was hiding a few yards away. But the bashing never came. No shouts of 'kurrah'. Nothing stirred. There was just an eerie silence. Others shuffled by as bemused as I was. I collected my mate and together we crept to the point where the guard house could be seen. Not a guard in sight. Could this be a trap? Waiting for something to happen so they had the excuse of opening fire on us?

The hated flag which usually hung draped at the bottom of the flagpole after sun down, had gone. Empty crates and rubbish strewn all over the place. I recall looking at each other in total disbelief. We entered into the open, every sinew in our body tensed, expecting the un-expected. Nothing happened. Still no guards. Then someone shouted ' the bastards have gone'. The words shot through the camp like a lit fuse. Then another voice yelled 'the trucks have gone' and so they had.

After a while a few natives appeared, telling us with gestures and much excitement that the guards indeed had gone during the night. Later we learned that the war had ended three days earlier on August 15. We wondered whether the Japs had known! I cannot begin to tell how this news was received by us. Some sank to their knees and prayed. Others just stood there, tears streaming down their haggard faces. A few were running around wildly gesticulating and screaming.

I could not grasp the enormity of what had happened. I had become a person again as sudden as it was ripped away from me, many long years ago. I remember the feeling of triumph that swept over me. I had done it! I had outlived all attempts by Hirohito and his murdering thugs to kill me. But, above all else, I could say NO again to anyone and anything. It is called freedom and democracy. Believe me, it is worth fighting for. The present and generations to come around our world, MUST be made aware of this so they can guard their birthrights with all their might.

However, a heavy shadow hung over the camp that day, because on the 16th. of August, a day after the war had officially ended, an Aussie friend was bayonetted to death by a Japanese guard. He had made an escape bid and was promptly returned to the camp by members of a nearby hill tribe. It was believed that the Japanese paid handsomely for this kind of enterprise. I only hope that his folk at home never found out.

We found a locomotive and some flat-tops in a nearby siding. After a short inspection of the loco we decided that the engine was serviceable and we began our journey South with great care and little progress. Then, after only a short while, a cry from the leading flat-top pierced the quiet air. OUR ORDEAL WAS OVER. A rescue train was slowly steaming up the track towards us. Two Red Cross flags flying at either side of the loco. The train had left a base camp a few days earlier, picking up survivors as it rattled up the track. They had been told about us, but did not know where we were and had begun to fear the worst. I do not recall having been given so many pills and injections in one day. But I do recall the warmth coursing through my veins swapping jokes with the medics, the feeling of belonging, to be among your own. I was eventually taken to the field hospital at Kanchanabury, where we were once again separated into groups of nationalities. I did not cherish this at all.

Life became pretty boring after that, whilst waiting to be repatriated. I managed to join the Military Police Corps which kept me reasonably occupied. On one occasion an event occurred which has stayed with me ever since. We used to frequent a Thai cafe for drinks, snacks and exchange news. The owner of the cafe had a little girl who had stolen our hearts in particular mine. This little girl fell seriously ill. The Thai doctor treating her said that he did not have the necessary drugs to treat her and that without those drugs she would die. We dragged our own doctor to the cafe to examine the little girl, with the Thai doctor in attendance.

He confirmed the Thai doctor's findings and agreed that without the required drugs she would indeed die. But, under the military rules at that time, he could not supply drugs of any kind to the Thai population. However, we understood the 'wink' and 'nod' and so I became a thief once more, this time with a medic as an accomplice. A close record was kept of the use of the drugs until the course was complete. The little girl made a full recovery. I have never had the slightest feeling of guilt about the way those drugs were obtained. I felt it was our 'thank you' to those Thai people who had risked their lives in trying to help us whenever they could. Needless to say that once the news got around, the local people were quite ready to accept us as their ruler, or so it seemed. This was a truly joyous time.

The aftermath of the Railway atrocities affected many POWs in different ways. Some showed minor problems, some were crippled for the rest of their lives. Others spent the rest of their days in hospital. Some suffered mental problems. A few could not handle the return to normal life and committed suicide, the most distressing fatality of all.

Still others saw their marriage torn apart, often because of a complete character change. I was one of the lucky ones. My problems were manageable though still with me today. The problems I had to deal with whilst working on the Railway were mainly chronic dysentery, intermittent malaria attacks, of which one was too close for comfort, minor beri-beri symptoms, pellagra and a small tropical ulcer which miracously healed. These ulcers were feared most by the POWs. They caused horrible limb disfigurement and often required amputation without an anaesthetic! But there was always the malnutrition problem, which caused such slaughter among the POWs. Many went blind as a result of prolonged vitamin deficiency. Others lost all their teeth as a result of chronic pellagra. My remaining problems are an enlarged spleen, an enlarged liver and a permanent disorder of the digestive system as a result of years of dysentery. On the whole I have managed very well in contrast to many of my old comrades who have led lives of misery since their return from hell. I had a little difficulty in adjusting to normal living and was treated by a psychiatrist for a while. Within a year of returning to normality I was ready to face the world again and that is what I did. One incredible point I have in common with other POWs still alive, we still have nightmares after more than half a century of civilised living. It would seem that the brain does not forget, however hard one tries to wipe out certain events. I can't make up my mind whether this is a good or bad thing. I have been encouraged on innumerable occasions by well meaning people to forgive and forget. I do not forgive, for it is not my right to forgive in the name of Harry, Bob, John, Kees, Digger, Lofty, Taffy, Shorty, Texas, Scotty, Paddy, my friends then, my friends still. They have a voice no more. I cannot forget for fear of omitting to alert the young of man's inhumanity to man.

There exist some events which still cause bitterness among surviving POWs.

1) In October 1946, the then British Government sold the Thai section of the Railway, together with most of the rolling stock to the Thai Government for £1,250,000.00 (Pound Sterling)The bulk of this money was used to recompense the owners of the rolling stock, locomotives and rails removed by the Japanese from Burma, Malaya and the Netherlands East Indies. (now Indonesia) It means that for every British corpse, lying in Thai soil, the then Government received £190.00. Spread over the total of Allied dead, this came to about £70.00 per corpse. A comforting thought indeed for the widows, relatives and other loved ones who lost their men folk in the jungles of Thailand and Burma.

2) The Japanese individual, captain Ishi, in command of the infamous UNIT 731 and responsible for the terrible biological trials carried out on Allied POWs and Asian civilians, made a deal with the Americans after the war, apparently in exchange for scientific biological data to the U.S.A. authorities. Ishi was not prosecuted as a war criminal. He died a few years later of cancer.

There now exists a memorial in Tokyo, dedicated to the officers and others who worked in UNIT 731. A memorial for the many victims of UNIT 731 does not exist!

3) Well documented sources have revealed that the Japanese Military High Command ordered their forces to eliminate all Allied POWs , at the end of August 1945. The bomb on Hiroshima prevented the unthinkable.

4) The San Francisco Peace Treaty of 1951 contained an escape clause in article 26 of the Treaty, allowing British ex-POWs to claim compensation in excess of the £76.50, allocated to them under the terms of the Treaty. Britain waived a very large proportion of its claim in order not to cripple the Japanese economy at the time. A Foreign Office directive stated that no publicity should be given to this decision. (Daily Telegraph, April 24, 1998).

5) During the latter half of 1944 and the early part 1945, large numbers of Allied POWs were transported to Japan from various locations in the Far East. The ships used for this purpose did not carry any markings indicating the presence of POWs aboard. As a consequence 18 Japanese vessels were sunk by Allied naval action. The total number of POWs transported on these ships was around 15,500. The total perished through Allied naval action was about 11,000. The great majority of these transports took place during the latter half of 1944.

Looking back at my time on the Railway, I feel in some way privileged to have endured this hell. It is given to few people to observe their fellow beings, stripped of the trappings of civilisation. The raw nature of man soon emerges, once the protective mantle of society is ripped away. I have observed men of immense stature in civilian life, crumble like dry earth when confronted with issues affecting their own life or that of their comrades. A truly pathetic and pitiful sight.

On the other hand, there was a man who had been the head master of an elementary school. A typical man for this job by appearance. Bald headed, with a fringe of hair at the back of his head. Slightly built of small stature, walking with a slight stoop. Always polite, always civil. The guards did not seem to bother him. He used to say: "It won't last for ever, they cannot possibly win this war. Just hang on and all will be all right in the end".

Then one day on the Railway, he jumped in front of a guard who was beating his sick friend. He shouted at the thug that if he wanted to beat up someone, he should at least have the courage to pick on a so called fit person. The guard proceeded to do just that with great abandon. The schoolmaster received a terrible beating. We had to carry him back to the camp that night. This timid, friendly little man rose to be a giant of mental strength, a beacon for us all to follow. We were separated later on and I have not heard from this marvellous man since. There are many examples like this, exposing human nature at its best and at its worst.

I firmly believe that nothing that life throws at an ex-POW, who has outlived the Thai-Burma Railway, can ever be as bad. It is a useful thought to keep alive.

There are those who, for reasons best known to themselves, will steadfastly deny the documented darker passages of history. To them I say: "Go and see the cemeteries in many countries in the Far East, where thousands upon thousands lie in eternal peace". These are not soldiers whose lives were snuffed out by a searching enemy bullet. These were defenseless, starving, sick, emaciated human beings, killed with intent. Through no fault of their own they became Prisoners of War. Go to these places, then if you have the courage, look me in the face and tell me: "It is not true. It never happened".

With this in mind, I quote the famous words : "When you go home, tell them of us and say, for your tomorrow we gave our today".

My words are:
....and when I came home I told them about us, the dead and the surviving.
They listened, they nodded, smiling, FORGETTING.
The widow held my hand, kissing me on the cheek, lightly, not to rouse the pain within and walked away, sadly, proudly.
YES....I told them about US when I came home.

I can only hope that my surviving comrades will be able to live out their remaining years content with the knowledge that they fought A JUST FIGHT, regardless of how trite and outdated such sentiment may appear today. We took everything the enemy could throw at us. We survived the war and we survived hell. It is my hope that future generations never have to face what we went through, but should the need arise, I hope they will be blessed with another such generation of men and women.